The Hedgemen of Herefordshire

Chapter One

~

The Hedgemens Wonky House

    Katie Kym was now 10 years of age, having always lived by the seaside, she went to a charming little Sea School located in a bustling fishing village, called Mumbles. The School was called Oystermouth, a school dominated by the trials and tribulations of the surrounding's blue waters. Endless golden layered, bejewelled sandy bays captivated many a wanderlust stranger, who would also become entranced, dazzled, by the warmth and timeless natural beauty of this unique, little village.

    The time has come at last, time, yes, now time for Katie Kym to leave this very special, endearing school, which has been a truly wonderful place for Katie Kym. A happy, magical place that would remain in Katie's memory for the rest of her life.

    There was no way on earth she wanted to leave the school or leave her friends, or let go of the brilliant, kind, sea school masters who had carefully harnessed all the pupils. Masters who had tried to make them understand, appreciate, and at the same time respect the sea world in which they were all so lucky to be near.

Katie Kym had learned, savoured, packed in all sorts of different weird but wonderful experiences. She particularly liked going out with her friends on the little sailing boats, if the sea winds blew, the little boats would whizz through the water, she also learned to swim in the ocean like any natural born mermaid, or sea creature. Often she would tell all her friends that she was the real mermaid, the others just being mere pretenders. Seeing her in the deep water, they all fully believed she was a real mermaid.

Katie successfully mastered the art of sailing her little boat in boisterous, choppy, wavy conditions which would have stopped most of us going anywhere near the water, or even boarding a vessel for that matter.

Steering the little dingy boat through the locks, she was like any other captain poised to protect her vessel through the small harbour marina, careful not to crash into any on coming sea traffic on the congested sea lanes.

Communicating with the coast guards on nautical terms, being naughty she liked to tease them with her Pan Pan, a special sea code, a call for help, much to the annoyance of other passing boats, who would kindly stop to offer her a tow - only to find out her vessel was miraculously working by the time they arrived to help. Katie would say, "sorry old chaps, ran out of fuel, fixed it now, the petrol fish came in the nick of time."

She would then descend to the lower deck, in fits of laughter, as there were no such petrol fish, swimming around carrying tanks of fuel. The slimy, slippery, underworld fishy creatures would slosh, splutter, roll around and play with her in the deep, dark, unyielding undercurrents of the Mixon waters.

Seals were her most enthusiastic playmates, Katie Kym would refer to these escapades as her sea seal dancing classes, in which she would always be flirting, looking for the next partner to take the next dance, ready to rock 'n roll with the drumming rhythms of the waves.

Showing not the slightest sign of fear, she was unphased by the unknown, Katie Kym relished and adored her special friends in this unspoilt, natural world. Having now been on many different adventures, along with her school chums, she had no idea what would happen next, for she was definitely going to be tip toeing into uncharted waters which were newly unknown to her, and which made her feel apprehensive for the first time in her life.

Free from any of life's fears, the realisation of the forthcoming wrench from the warmth of the bay had hit her like a brick, Katie now felt absolutely petrified. The last day of the school term had gone far too quickly, time to go home, time to leave the seaside, time to leave Oystermouth, certainly time to say goodbye to all of her friends.

Katie Kym wanted today to last forever. No day could last forever and she knew that, but she still could not control the inner bodily hosepipes that oozed floods of water out of her delicate, fresh, emerald green eyes. Her parents had arrived all too quickly at the school gate, ready to collect Katie Kym. By now everybody had cuddled each other for the last time, said their goodbyes, and promised to stay in touch with each other, always.

The highly electric, energised, 'leaving school' atmosphere had even sent the lollipop man into floods of throat locking emotions. He too could not stop the tears that were streaming down his chubby, round, cheeks.

Like many of the others leaving the school that day, all his little water babies were finally going, flying off to other nests. He had given every one of them a good luck letter that he had wrapped around a packet of sea-bug sweets that had been made of the finest rag-worms, full of protein, wonderful for growing little humans, a really tasty seaside treat.

The children loved them, especially if the sweet contained loads of the rag-worms' legs, the more legs the better for that honeycombe crunch.

One by one they gave him their last hug, Katie Kym had whispered in the old man's ear, "goodbye Lollipop Daddy, thank you for taking care of me, thank you for being here every day for us, love you Lollipops, love you." The old Lollipop man retired to the rickety old bench, today had really got the better of him, he just sat and cried quietly wishing them all the best of luck, as some of them would need it.

Dudley dig it, the scruffy cocker dog, was perched sitting upright in the back of the car, waiting for Katie Kym, black, fully-flared nostrils snorting through the tiny unclosed gap where the window had been left slightly open. The scruffy dog looked a mess, he never combed his own hair, his paws were far too big, his legs were far too long, his tail hadn't been docked and wagged continuously like a motorised sweeping brush that had been left on automatic.

Dad frequently threatened to sell the scruffy mutt. He would call the poor dig it dog the 'worst buy of the century', even to the point of writing a newspaper advert - 'One Dudley dig it, scruffy dog for sale, all because my daughter, known as Katie Kym, was far too lazy, far too busy to take enough care of her demented, canine pet'.

There had been many lively ding-dong discussions about the Demented, scruffy dog, let alone the sweeping motorised brushing tail, the massive black snotty nose, that left a continuous mess all over the car windows. It was this, that had been the catalyst for a family ding-dong to erupt. Dudley just did his best to ignore the insults, he would wind them up further, make things even worse by kissing them with that disgusting, huge, slimy, wet, pink tongue, which grated like sandpaper across your face. The more they would all shout, the more he would lick, Dudley would react to the rising noise levels with frantic panting, licking sessions, lick, lick, lick, dripping mucus, spraying his audience.

This guaranteed Dudley a wet victory, which succeeded in to quietening them all down into submission, then they would all shut up, horrified at the sheer mess the awful mutt had made.

Katie Kym reluctantly climbed into the back of the car; Dudley as ever was deliriously happy. His wet, disgusting, sloppy, panting tongue, once again splattered itself all over the rear windows, splattered all over Katie Kym, and then, just as anticipated the awful ritual licking session of the furry pest went into overdrive.

Katie Kym blasted, "go to sleep! Go to sleep you horrible snotty dog!" Dudley just smiled showing his pearly white teeth, and gently placed his head on Katie Kym"s lap, then at once, went to sleep as the car started to move. It rolled slowly down the main road and out of Mumbles, for the very last time that summer. The journey to their new home, coupled with the long unwanted journey to view her new house and school, was well underway. They had all been in the car for what seemed like hours when at last they arrived in a small country hamlet, smack in the middle of the Hedgemen country.

What do you do in the countryside? There's nobody about. Where have all the people gone? Where are the shops? Endless questions were whizzing through Katie's head, whizzing questions she did not know the answers to.

For a start, the house was ridiculously wonky; it looked as if it was going to fall down, the gardens were so overgrown with trees, hedges, and plants she had never seen before, Katie Kym could not believe they would all be moving into this horrid place, it was a gut-numbing shock. Getting to the horrid house had certainly been a bumpy ride, the drive was full of pot-holes and smothered with overgrown brambles.

Katie Kym had convinced herself nobody had lived here for years, it was Spooky, with a capital S. Rubbing her clammy brow she wanted to know what had happened to her sea, where had it gone? Her beautiful, beloved sea seemed so far away now. Yes, she had already made up her mind she would return there as soon as possible, Dudley dig it would show her the way home, her real seaside home.

They continued up the long pot-hole ridden, overgrown grounds, the house looked even bigger, even wonkier, creepy, creepy, wonky house. Finally, the engine of the car was switched off, there was an eery silence, Katie Kym felt nauseous and her stomach was churning slowly. She told herself that she would feel better when she had a little fresh air after getting out of the car, they had been on a long journey for some two and half hours, indeed most of the afternoon.

Quickly she opened the passenger door, the scruffy, demented, dig it dog was first out, leaping straight over Katie Kym, then he bolted into the distant greenery, she had no choice but to go immediately and take care of Dudley dig it.

Dudley getting lost, Dudley getting too excited, infuriated Katie Kym, she knew he could run for miles, absorbing all the new smells, stopping to dig the most enormous holes, searching for the under life! She wished he would get lost for good, for by now she had had enough of the scruffy, snotty nosed pest.

Weaving her way through the overgrown grounds, Katie Kym felt overwhelmed, her continuing jelly shock had subsided only mildly, she started calling for Dudley. " Come back here you bad dog. Come back at once you horrid dog!" Dudley had disappeared through the dense overgrowth, all she could do now was call tirelessly. She even tried whistling like a boy in an unlady-like manner.

The more Katie Kym searched, the denser the overgrowth and foliage became, no natural pathways, just rampant, clambering green overgrowth. "Dudley, come back, come back, here now! For the last time come back!" shouted Katie. Still no response from Dudley, her wish that he should get lost had now been granted.

Not a wimp, not a whinge, not even a snooty snort, this situation had completely disorientated Katie, she had totally lost her bearings, her rising temper, the constant hissing did not help matters, she was hyperventilating with anger.

Deciding to turn around, she tried to go back the way she had come; from the wonky house, that ridiculous wonky house. A Rustling in the bushes distracted her, she was absolutely panic stricken being out here alone. Katie Kym had quite naturally assumed the rustling noise was at last Dudley who was just messing about, getting his own back.

Katie Kym peered into the bushes, she could not see Dudley or hear any of the grunting, piggy, mutt noises. Going a little deeper, deeper, this big, prickly, dark, black hedge, had scratched her leg with one of its nasty jagged thorns, one of them embedded itself into her lower leg, like a dagger.

Her leg bled, she just kept wiping the wounded area, the pain had been sharp, a real stab. Jellyfish stings yes, razor fish wounds, she had encountered those before, but this had been a nasty attack, a really nasty jab of rustic country.

Without any warning, and unable to see the culprit, Katie Kym could hear a nasty voice, saying, "serves you right, serves you right." Looking all around and around, but still not seeing the culprit, Katie imagined that it was not a thorn that had penetrated her leg but some other dark invader which had spiked her. As quickly as she could she hurled herself out of the bushes, panicked by the fact that what ever that horrible thing was, it could talk. Yuk! Yuk! Yuk! Yucky thing, what ever it was, she no longer had the desire to find out!

Fleeing back to the old house, absolutely scared out of her wits, Katie ran like the clappers, annoyed but then relieved to see Dudley who had also returned back home safely. She wondered if he too had been harmed by the talking, dark, unseable black stabber. Her heart was thumping and pumping really fast with fright.

After closer inspection Dudley had returned not even the slightest bit ruffled, nor in the slightest bit bothered that she had been attacked by a talking thorn. Dudley knew Katie Kym would exaggerate, she always did when she found herself in trouble.

This was the last straw for Katie, it was true, Dudley was her worst friend, that dog, that scruff, could stay out all night for all she cared, he would never be allowed to stay in her new bedroom, he could sleep outside with the talking thorn.

Leaning on the outside arch at the rear entrance of the house, her father noticed Katie Kym, hissing, hobbling, holding tight to her wounded leg. Observing his daughter's injury, the first blood cut, though he was sure there would be many others as time went on, he smiled to himself, part and parcel of being young, adventurous and carefree, he thought. Loudly he said, "not looking where you were going little child?" Clearly Dudley would be in the dog house continuously at this rate as things had got off to a bad start for his girl.

Katie Kym could hardly breathe, she scrambled to tell him everything that had happened to her in the bushes,

Dad reassured her, told her not to worry, the hedges would be sorted out, and sorted out they would be, once he had found the time in between all the other jobs.

Katie Kym, said, "Dad, you do not seem too concerned about my leg, or the talking nasty talking culprit thorn that did it to me." "I am concerned about your leg Katie, and I am concerned about the talking thorn." "Well what was it Dad?" demanded Katie Kym. Softly he answered her probing questions, "one of the Hedgemen." "The Hedgemen," she asked curiously, "one of the Hedgemen of Herefordshire, they all live out here and protect the countryside. It's nice to know that they are still out here Katie Kym." 'They', she thought. "How many would you say are out there then Dad?" "You'll just have to go back into the garden to find out for yourself Katie Kym. It is for you to find out, with Dudley, the next time you both go out."

Katie Kym ran into the house looking for her mother, "Mum - Dad said there were men living in the Hedges, lots of different ones, not very nice either, not very nice at all, one of the nasty, talking creeps has stabbed me, look Mum, look, the creep has stabbed me!" Mum just laughed, "Oh dear Katie Kym, what are we going to do with your old Dad, he has finally gone potty. I'll call the Doctor tomorrow, that should sort him out, along with the men in white coats. Talking Hedgemen! What will he think of next. I'm sure it's the funny tea he's been drinking a lot of lately, he really is out of his box." Katie Kym started to think her Mum had been right, Dad had gone potty, but what did she mean 'out of his box', even she had heard voices coming from the hedges. Maybe she was going potty too, or perhaps she too had lost her box, what ever that was, or may be, just maybe, Mum was potty, because she did not have a box, and she certainly did believe anything you told her.

Katie recalled the time when she told her Mum about what the sea creatures once told her, that she was a real mermaid, a Mumbles' mermaid. Thinking about this made Katie Kym feel very tired and sad, it was now getting late, time for bed, this day had gone on for ever. Upstairs, tucked nicely into bed, Katie Kym drifted in and out of sleep, a tapping noise on the small leaded window pane kept her awake. Dad entered the room to say his final good night. "Dad! Dad! What's that tapping?" she whispered in his ear. "Oh! It's only Rosie Hip calling Mr Pole and the rest of the Hedgemen of Herefordshire! Go to sleep now - go to sleep." Katie started thinking, Rosie Hip - who on earth is Rosie Hip? Who is Mr Pole? What do they all look like? Where are the other Hedgemen? Hiding! She fell into a long, deep, delirious sleep, trying to envisage what they truly looked like.

Chapter Two

~

Rosie Hip, Captain Privet, and The Golden Nut

Rosie Hip is young, just like Katie Kym. She is budding; she is beautiful; adventurous and extraordinary for such a delicate bud. Rosie lives in a very old and established country garden, adjacent to the wonky house, the black and white house that Katie Kym has just moved into. Rosie looks different and lives a different life to that of Katie Kym, because Rosie lives outdoors, amidst the scented honeysuckle.

The garden you may see outside your house changes all the time, but Rosie hardly ever does. Her outdoor winter coat is a magnificent deep rich crimson red. It keeps Rosie warm and dry during the long, cold, wet and windy winter months. She never takes her red coat off in the winter season. If ever she lost her coat, Rosie would not survive; she would never be able to go out again; she would shrivel up and fade away, into the compost heap like some of her long lost friends.

Indeed, only a few people have seen Rosie Hip without her winter coat, which she can take off for a limited time, but only on very special days of the year, which are mainly in the summer months. Her enchanting face, her own delicate designer haute-couture in summertime, is just something so special. Therefore it is not surprising that all the villagers know Rosie Hip is very delicate and unique, totally different to what Katie Kym could have ever imagined.

Rosie Hip really does need taking care of in a special way. Rosie will not willingly reveal herself to just anybody, only those she knows and trusts: those who would be able to look after her and protect her eternal secrets, at all times, whatever the circumstances may entail.

Only the elite squad, these being the robustly powerful Hedgemen of Herefordshire, really know what Rosie looks like. They are always calling on Rosie; any excuse, any excuse, any excuse; just to have another glimpse at Miss Hip's very unusual beauty. They are all extremely protective of her: Rosie is one of their best-kept well-hidden friends. The Captain has no doubt she is a natural treasure that will remain a hidden secret forever; he will never stop protecting her because that's his job, and he's jolly pleased to do it.

Captain Willie Privet lives right next door to Rosie Hip. He is one the worst offenders for popping in and out of Rosie Hip's house all the time. Privet is somewhat overbearing, to say the least. He never stops pestering Rosie; because apart from this being his job, he has fallen head over heals in love with Rosie Hip, but he does not know how to tell her, how ever could he.

All night long Privet never stops; he is always on guard duty.

He keeps a look-out for unwanted guests, 'the enemy' he calls them. He is continuously calling out for the other Hedgemen to help him. He is always calling on Rosie Hip, just to make sure she has not had any unwanted visitors, such as some of the other Hedgemen, who he suspects would take Rosie Hip away from him as they too have fallen in love with her.

Today is Sunday. Rosie Hip feels she might get a little rest today; she feels she may stay indoors and keep warm, as the summer has just gone! No such luck - all of a sudden Captain Willie Privet starts his pestering again.

"Rosie Hip! Rosie Hip! Wake up!" demanded the Captain. "Wake up! Wake up! Have you seen that new girl, who has just moved into our house? Her name is Katie Kym, you know; she has this dog called Dudley! I've not got all day; if you don't come out now, I will not tell you all the latest news about her. Neither will I tell you what she calls the poor dog, with her stomping bad temper. I've never heard the likes of it; you did not dare talk like that in my day. That's the trouble with these human children; they have not been brought up like we were."

Like all army captains, he liked the sound of his own voice. It made him feel good, really good! The louder he shouted, the better he felt.

"Get out here now, Rosie Hip. I will most certainly accompany you this morning, otherwise you will be left all alone to face that funny dog and the exceedingly bad tempered Katie Kym."

Rosie Hip rolled her big blue eyes around; round, round and around. His loud voice had sent shockwaves pulsating through her delicate little head. The nagging old Captain should be put on the compost heap, she thought. The noise had been unbearable, with his persistent, repetitive parrot like voice which irritated Rosie Hip to bits, especially at this time of the morning, it was far too early. The garden birds had only just started warming up for the Dawn Chorus, and she had not warmed up at all. She had completely forgotten that she had promised to go for a walk with the Captain, down to the dirty, dirty, dumblehole. The new family that had moved into the wonky house had also distracted her; she really and truly had forgotten.

Rosie Hip was not too keen to go down to the dirty dumblehole. There was a lot of water there, and "where there's water, there's mud." But there had been a whisper of something quite special at the dumblehole, yes a little whisper! Something something, they would all have to search for.

Rosie Hip certainly did not want to miss out, not in the slightest, no matter how dirty the place seemed, she would just have to help find something, of course this morning she would just have to grin and bear it. Oh dear! Oh dear! Oh dear she thought. Where there's mud, there's a mess, a mess and another mess! This means mud on my red coat, my only red coat. Oh no! Oh no! And she panicked, hoping this outing would be over sooner rather than later. She couldn't possibly get her only red coat muddy, dirty, wet, muddy what ever, No! No, no, no! No chance whatsoever, because if ever she did this, it would be the end of Rosie Hip; then she would never have a chance of making friends with the new girl Katie Kym, let alone meet her for the first time, she longed to have a new friend, a real friend.

Rosie Hip rustled towards the Captain. The exaggerated drooping mouth, the shocked, rubbery expression on his face; they said it all. Nobody could fail to notice Rosie Hip. He scratched his head, pondering as to why she always looked so wonderful in that bright clean red coat. He worried that she was far too noticeable. He had no doubt that in time others would find out about them, their cover would be blown. Her red coat looked like a walking radar beacon because it was just so bright, too bright for this part of the countryside, especially when one has no desire to be seen, no desire what so ever.

Sometimes this put him and the others in a very difficult position, a very difficult awkward quandary in fact, being the keepers of the countryside and especially all being members of the country side secret service. Once again he had second thoughts about taking her on this dangerous mission. But there was nothing he could do about it now, as he had promised to take her and he loved her.

Anybody that lived in the thick, dense Herefordshire countryside always wore green or brown, the coded colours of the elite squad. You would hardly notice them rushing and rustling, in and out of the hedges, doing their daily duties, carrying out orders, being absolutely discreet, and making sure they were unseen and unheard.

The Captain started his usual mutterings to himself: mutter, mutter, murmuring mutterings. I really must watch out for Rosie; it's quite dangerous for her, quite dangerous! For the third time, he wished he had not asked her on this outing. Oh dear! Oh, what should I do? They will all spot her, they will all find out; then their cover would be blown, and he would be in serious trouble. This was going to be far too risky; he could lose his job - then what?

"Morning Captain", Rosie sweetly said, staring at him.

He stood in front of Rosie, looking like a strong and forthright protective hero. Her big blue eyes, her innocent pink lips, made the Captain all of a quiver. There was no way he could upset Rosie Hip; she was a truly beautiful English rose.

"Glad to see you dressed for our morning outing, Rosie. Come along, come along! Come along, hurry it up! We cannot be late this morning, Rosie. We cannot be late as the others will be waiting for us, even now."

They both hurried down the winding steps, which led from the garden onto the small, narrow lane. The dumblehole lane, with its tightly-packed hedgerows, was at its best this time of the year, full of exotic wild fruits and pungent country smells. However, once you had reached the bottom of the lane then you could not miss the dirty, mucky dumblehole.

Just as Rosie Hip had suspected: lots of water, lots of dirt, lots of mud, lots of water, dirty muddy water. She flinched; all the muscles in her body flinched, just dreading the thought of spoiling her shiny red coat which would be dulled by getting it wet. It had all gone so well up to now, as she liked the walk down the pretty scented lane.

"Rosie, you go across the bridge quickly," the Captain ordered. "I'll follow you in a few moments."

The water under the bridge had started to rise; it was getting deeper and deeper. At this time of the year, the dumblehole flooded very quickly, as the rainfall made its way down the hilly ravines, down to the dumblehole into the now fast-flowing stream. Should you slip in, it was a mighty dangerous place to be on your own if you could not swim, a mighty dangerous place. Rosie Hip comforted herself by the fact that she was with the Hedgemen and she would not be alone, she would soon find what the something was that they were searching for.

Finally she crossed the bridge, but did not like it in the slightest. Her leafy green boots started to get wet, dirty and sticky. A difficult place to come for a morning's outing she thought; a funny old place. Not so funny if she got stuck in the awful, dirty, muddy water, not so funny if she were to get her leafy boots any wetter as they would just fall off her tiny feet and float down stream. No; not funny at all.

Rosie Hip huffed, and started to think about Katie Kym. She did not have to wear leafy boots. Indeed, she dressed quite peculiarly for a girl moving into the country. Rosie Hip decided she would have to make her a pair of leafy boots, so she too could go out with her into the countryside, perhaps, just perhaps on their next outing.

The wind had started to pick up, which made that horrid bridge even worse. It started to sway and wobble, wobble blowing side to side in the windy gust. Rosie Hip started to wobble and wobble with the movement of the bridge. She did not like this sensation in the slightest. She felt sure that one more blow, one more wobble and she would end up going downstream, like her green leafy boots, washed away, never to be seen again, as she could not swim at all.

Forgetting about the wobbles she became distracted completely, by the sheer numbers of sticklers out. What on earth are they all doing here? she wondered. They were all jumping about, jumping about looking extremely glum. Rosie Hip felt sorry for them: what on earth had happened to all their green uniforms? Some of the sticklers ended up in the stream and just floated around forever; they had lost their homes. Where had the uniforms gone? What had they done with them? They were bare sticks. Rosie Hip could not believe they would dare go outdoors without getting dressed. This is quite an appalling way to behave, she thought. Oh dear! They'll get into trouble now; they will catch a death with the cold.

The Captain burst out laughing; he could not stop laughing. Privet always found the sticklers most amusing. Stupid sticks, he thought; stupid, stupid sticks; they need throwing to the dogs, or burning like the other dead wood in these parts. If only they would follow his instructions; then they wouldn't keep losing their uniforms and getting into trouble.

"Rosie, do not concern yourself with the likes of those sticklers," he said. "They ought to know about the secrets in the countryside by now. They never take orders; they are not like you and me, you know. They get up to all sorts. It serves them right, stupid sticks; just serves them right. Common little sticks, common little troublemakers who lower the tone of our garden and mess it up. They are stick louts. Yes, stick louts!"

Rosie turned and looked away from the Captain. She nearly jumped out of her coat at the sight of Commander Blackthorn.

"Oh, what are you doing here?" she gasped, almost speechless as she could hardly get any air, struck by the sight of the ghastly black little creep.

The Commander had summoned the Captain to the

dumblehole as he had become very concerned about all the coming and goings in the little village. Strangers to these parts of the country had started to arrive in large numbers, with cars, plastic bags and litter rubbish, which they would discard in our hedges.

"These strangers are taking things from our village that don't belong to them," said the Commander. "They think they can just waltz in and take what they like." The people living in the village had been asking Mr Pole to use the bush telegraph service to contact the Hedgemen of Herefordshire and ask for further help, as there were too many of them. Over the last few weeks the problem had worsened. The Commander knew why they had come, and he knew who they were.

"They must be stopped before it's too late," said the Commander, "otherwise this will certainly be the end of the Hedgemen. We are all in danger now. We must think of some way to get rid of the unwanted strangers in the village."

Rosie looked even more troubled. She knew that these people came year after year, but even she had to admit that there seemed to be a lot more this year. She overheard the Captain telling the Commander: "We must make a move to stop them, otherwise they will all be gone, all be gone, and there will be trouble ahead. There will be nothing left if that lot keep nicking from our village, pillaging ignorant greedy litter-dropping people."

Then Major Conker called out to Rosie, which made Rosie blush. Her heart started to flutter; her eyes started to flutter - like a butterfly. She could not stop fluttering in front of Major Conker. The big strong Major, being so round and muscular, would sort them out for sure, she thought; along with the sharp creepy Commander's help.

"Miss Hip," he said. "Commander Blackthorn insists that I now escort you home." "Well, we have only just got here, Major," cried Rosie.

"Don't upset yourself, Miss Hip, but I must get you home with some urgency. Come, we will have to leave right now. Hurry!"

Rosie Hip looked even more puzzled than ever, and worried again as she thought about the swaying wobbly, wobbly bridge. The wind had got worse too; things were blowing all over the place. The sticklers had all started shouting for Captain Privet. "Help! Help! Help!" They were quite frantic. The gusty wind was blowing even harder; there was a commotion down at the dumblehole. The weather had turned nasty very quickly, and some of the sticklers had already fallen into the fast moving stream.

Major Conker took hold of Rosie's hand. As she turned to follow him, something hard hit her on the back of her head; something very hard, which almost sent her tumbling into the water. It was a good job the Major had held firmly onto her cute little hand; she had been saved by the Major! Yes! Rosie Hip loved her hero the strong, handsome Major.

"Oh, what was that?" squeaked Rosie Hip.

She turned around to look. Quickly the Major, the Commander and the Captain all gathered around Rosie Hip to look at what had hit her, and to make sure Rosie Hip was alright.

"There it is, there it is, there it is," the Captain said. "Pick it up, pick it up, Commander pick it up."

"Found it, Captain," said the Commander. "Found it, got it, got it. No wonder these people are coming here. At least we have got here first."

Rosie Hip still did not know what they had all found. She had not got a clue what had hit her! She did not see it, whatever it was. The Captain quickly put the round, hard, small object into Rosie's pocket.

"Hide it, hide it, hide it, Rosie," he muttered. "Get home quickly now with the Major, as fast as you can."

They both rushed and rushed, as quickly as they could, without spoiling Rosie's red coat. Her leafy boots were very dirty and battered, she made a mental note never to go there again in those boots. She would have to make a new pair; she would use maple leaf next time.

Having got back to Rosie Hip's house safely, ruffled, but quite breathlessly exhausted, they were both extremely tired and very thirsty.

"Major Conker," Rosie gasped. "I am so thirsty I need a drink after all that."

She poured herself and the Major a long, chilled special hip syrup juice, made a long time ago by her adoring grandmother. After a couple of glasses of the special syrup juice, Rosie felt much better; much, much better, quelling her thirsts and nerves at the same time. She had almost forgotten about the thing in her pocket. What had she got in her pocket? Rosie Hip still had no idea, it must be that something.

Captain Willie Privet barged into Rosie's house, looking completely flushed, angry at all the strangers he had passed on the way. He was in no mood for Granny's hip syrup. Rosie Hip insisted he should have just a small one: all this stress was bad for him, he was far too old for these sorts of shenanigans, but it had to be done for all their benefit.

But the only thing the Captain was interested in was the thing in Rosie Hip's pocket which was hidden deep in her shiny red coat. He urgently wanted it; and he wanted it now.

"Rosie, may I have what is in your pocket? Would you care to give it to me now?"

Rosie hesitated.

"Give it to me! Give it to me now!" the Captain firmly demanded.

So she put her hand in her pocket, and gave the Captain this funny-looking shiny, round thing.

"What is it, Captain? What is it?"

Rosie Hip had never seen one of these before; not this bright, golden-coloured, rounded object. The Captain was quick to answer.

"A golden King Cobb nut Rosie. A secret golden nut," he said, clasping the nut and rubbing the palm of his strong shiny hand. "A secret golden king nut. These nuts are extremely rare, Rosie. They only grow in special places, like Herefordshire."

It had been a hundred years since the last ones were found, a long hundred years. So they were very excited finding this golden nut, and news of this extraordinary find had already quickly spread to all of the other villagers, who knew the village harboured many untold secrets. Outside they were all waiting to see it. The Captain and the Major had other ideas: the villagers were not going to be allowed to get anywhere near it, let alone see it.

The Captain ordered Rosie to close the curtains, for the contents of the golden nut had not yet been revealed to anybody; they must remain a Herefordshire secret. The Major helped Rosie to put the nut in a special wooden box. The Captain then opened it up in front of them. Rosie Hip just froze with delight. She could hardly believe what was inside the bright, shimmering shell.

"Oh, oh, oh! My, my! It's beautiful!" Rosie exclaimed. "I want that, I want that! I'm having that! I must have that, I must have that, I must have that now, Captain! Please can I have it, Captain? Please may I?"

The Captain smiled at Rosie, brushing that big moustache of his with his hands, removing the dishevelled whiskers that covered his mouth.

"Only if you promise never to tell anybody else, Rosie, about the golden nut; not even that new girl called Katie Kym who has just moved in - nobody apart from the Major and myself, Rosie, who already know about them. Do you understand, Rosie? Do you fully understand, Rosie?"

Rosie nodded her tiny head in agreement with the Captain. He raised his eyebrows, and left Rosie's house with Major Conker, giving Rosie Hip the secret golden nut to look after safely. This just being another excuse for the Captain to keep calling on her and checking out their new secret.

Rosie was so excited; all day long she had been excited. She wanted to tell Katie Kym, but she knew that she would never be able to tell anybody. She wanted to contact Mr Pole's bush telegraph service, just to let a few friends know about the outing with the Captain, Major Conker, the sticklers, the wobbly bridge, the dirty wet muddy dumblehole. There was a lot Rosie Hip wanted to say but could not, which was a shame, as this had been such a wonderful and exciting outing, a very special day.

The Captain and the Major knew she would tell some of her other friends, bits and bobs about today's outing. They both smiled, for they knew and trusted Rosie Hip with their golden secret. They could not believe Rosie Hip had actually agreed to go out with them in the first instance to such a dangerous place; especially in that beautiful red coat of hers. The golden nuts have many secrets, and the Hedgemen of Herefordshire know what they are. Also, they knew that Rosie Hip would never tell a soul about finding the secret golden nut, or what the secret nut had revealed; let alone tell anybody where it had been found.

The Captain tucked himself into bed, ready for another day. Tomorrow was going to be busy, busy, very busy indeed, as the news had spread, even though at this point it was pure speculation on the part of those who didn't really know the true story.

Rosie too felt tired and went to bed, with the golden nut firmly in her pocket. Today, for once, she adored Captain Privet; she would have to stop wishing he would go to the compost heap - he had been so kind to her all day. Rosie Hip adored the Major too: she wanted to go out with him again. Tomorrow she would thank them both for letting her look after the secret golden nut.

All night long Rosie tossed and turned. A few times she woke up, so she could look at the golden nut glowing in the darkness of the night. It just glowed and glowed and glowed. This was amazing! What had they really all found? Why had they found it now? What was the purpose of having a secret golden nut?

Just like Katie Kym, Rosie Hip was very inquisitive, always asking herself questions, not really knowing any of the answers, which she could only guess at.

Chapter Three

~

Faro The Rainbow Man

Rosie Hip woke after a restless night, startled by the dazzling and rare appearance of the ever-rolling sunball. The sun just dazzled, dazzled, dazzled: and so brightly that the dark winter sky had become engulfed in a blanket of the warm, orange blaze, like a fire that warms a cold room on a winter's night.

Katie Kym had also awoken and proceeded to get ready for another day at her new school, listening to the chirping squatters who have nested in the attic of her new bedroom. The March equinox had long passed. The Equinox happens on two special days in the year when night and day are of equal lengths: twelve hours of night, twelve hours of light. Katie Kym had always been joyous with the longer days, as this had meant she would not be forced to go to bed too early. Katie liked staying up late, the equinox being a good excuse to argue her case: How can you go to sleep when it's daylight? She dragged the remainder of the long summer days out to her advantage, but unfortunately, these long days would not last forever.

Dudley, the batty, demented dog, picked up on Katie's protracted gloom. Dudley could do nothing for Katie Kym; even tantalising her with his wet sandpaper tongue did not lift her spirits. He would lie in his kennel watching the newly spawned family of mice nibbling at his biscuits. He did not mind, at least Dudley had another family to keep him company in his dreary, cold doghouse.

Rosie Hip had no intention of getting up yet. Once again she was shattered from the excitement of the day before. The Hedgemen of Herefordshire had left her in a dizzy, dizzy world of her own. Often at this time of the year Rosie would sleep all day, as winter days in Herefordshire were long, dark and foggy - foggy, foggy and extremely yucky, yucky, yucky, and predominantly mucky; mucky, mucky and very, very yucky. And then there had been the dirty, wet, windy yesterday, when she had gone out.

She had no intention of getting her wonderful red coat covered in the wet, mucky, yucky, foggy blanket. Yesterday was enough, she thought, quite enough, but at least she had ended up with the secret golden nut. This would keep her very occupied for the rest of the day, as she had no idea what she should really be doing with it.

Rosie Hip looked at the big wooden house next door; she lived on the outside of it, on the wall that faced east. The house looked almost sad and empty. Well it had been sad, and it had been empty until Katie Kym had moved in with her dog.

A fantastic, luminous rainbow had now eclipsed the entire wonky house. Rosie Hop became ecstatic as it had certainly been a long time since the Rainbow Man had shown and flashed his colours. She watched as the end of his long, multi-coloured coat tail settled at the bottom of the garden. Some people in the village say that when you find the end of a rainbow there is a pot of gold waiting to be collected by the lucky finder. Rosie Hip knew that at the end of hers a multi-coloured man would appear wearing a funny hat, but he was far more interesting than a pot of gold.

Rosie hip knew that it would be sometime before she would have another outing with Captain Privet and the Major. The wintertime keeps everybody busy; busy with keeping warm and dry. And being busy, busy, busy doing things meant that they did not have time for too many outings. But this of course may change, thought Rosie, now that I have the secret golden nut - and Faro, The Rainbow Man has returned to the garden. Why, she pondered?

But all of a sudden a big, black cloud darkened her room. The sun had disappeared; the wonderful orange sky went very dark and then it started to pour with rain. Splattering rain, splashing rain, splatter, splatter, splash, splash.

"Oh no! Oh no, not again!"

Rosie Hip looked out of her leafy window in despair. She was fully awake now, and with the splashing and splattering came the wind, its thundering, thumping just echoing louder and louder.

"Oh no! Oh no! Not another of those dreadful winter clatter-banging, windy storms!"

The continuation of the recent storms had been most unusual for this time of the year. They were sending shockwaves everywhere and causing havoc in the garden. Trees had fallen, leaves had gone, Rosie did not feel safe in her home, she was getting very worried. The torrential rain had caused the fishpond to flood and the fish were swimming all over the grass. It was a mess, it was chaos, and she could do little to help the fish; she only hoped that they would be able to swim back into their cosy pond once the storm was over.

There was a mighty bang, a second mighty bang and Rosie jumped, and jumped again.

"Goodness me! That was a frightful clatter-banger! When will they stop it? When will they stop causing so much damage?" Wailed Rosie.

Then the black sky disappeared, the rain stopped, and dancing bright sunshine returned. Rosie Hip looked through the window with sheer relief that the storm had come to an end. It was all due to temperature, really; temperature, you see, is another one of life's complications, temperature/temper, what's the difference?

Rosie Hip had no wish to bother with the hot and cold physics of the elements. Quickly getting dressed she put on her lovely red coat and watched as her coat turned green. Then it turned orange, then it turned yellow, then it turned blue, then it turned purple, then it turned pink. Rosie Hip started to tremble once again.

"What had happened to my red coat?" She started to yell, to shout out really loud. "My redcoat! My lovely red coat has gone pink! It has gone pink!"

Tears were streaming, rolling all the way down her cheeks. A pink coat! A pink coat! She did not want a pink coat! Rosie Hip sobbed, sobbed and sobbed. She wanted her red coat back: where had it disappeared to? Rosie almost collapsed in utter despair: she would never be able to replace her red coat now. She was going to die, without ever seeing the Major again - her coat had gone and she was convinced that she would die without it. "Oh!", she cried. "I am doomed, I've lost my coat."

Then a large, funny looking blue hand stroked her face gently, wiping away the stream of tears. A softly spoken voice called out to her. Looking up she could hardly see a thing. She raised her head again and all she could see with her bleary vision was a tall, willowy man of different colours. Rosie recognised instantly this funny, multi-coloured man, and a broad smile surfaced on her now happy little face.

"Rosie! Rosie, what on earth is the matter?" queried Faro the Rainbow Man as he made his way up to the house from the bottom of the garden.

"My red coat has turned pink! I do not want a pink coat!", protested Rosie. "No Rosie! It has not!" Said Faro quietly.

Rosie looked again. Faro was absolutely right. Her coat was red, very red, very red. Everything changes colour when the Rainbow Man calls; all objects become a coloured illusion, honestly, why did she always forget!

Faro had disappeared when she looked up again; his trail of

colour laminated the big, wooden, wonky house. It had not taken him long to light up every window - one blue window, one yellow window, one green window, one red window, one purple window, one pink window, enchanting - enchanting the wooden wonky house, a dream of wonderful colours, a dream of a house.

Rosie Hip could not wait to tell him about what they had found the previous day at the dumblehole, though she had promised the Captain that she would not tell a soul. But Faro was different. He was Mr Rainbow Whizz. He looked different from Rosie and her friends; peculiar really, quite peculiar. There again rainbow people do look different, but you could trust them with your secrets, even secrets of a golden nut, because the Rainbow Whizzard was a keeper of secrets, and besides, he had lots of his own secrets which he told Rosie from time to time.

He explained many times to Rosie Hip, and many times to the Hedgemen, as to why he looked so different, and why he could come and go as he pleased, though sometimes he did not have much choice. He also explained about his ancestors, he being the son of a family whose ancestors originated from the deep African spiritual region, Dogon of Mali.

His descendent was a twin called Pembra, who originated from a neighbouring African country, the spiritual region of Bambara. It was said that Pembra's ancestors made the earth, while his identical twin made the sky. Then the first grass grew, the first waters appeared and the twins became one, known as Faro.

Rosie Hip often found this family tree business too difficult to understand. After all, everybody's family tree is different, she thought. It became even more confusing when she considered that we have all come from different backgrounds and different origins. She would never understand it, this was all far too complicated, far too complicated for Rosie Hip, a country secret, living quietly in the countryside, outdoors.

One thing she did completely understand: Faro would not stay here for long. He always had to return to the sky for long periods of time.

Making her way to the wonky house Rosie began to tap on the carved oak door of the wooden house: Tap, tap, tap. Faro opened the door. His hat, his fluorescent clothes were like the brightly lit rainbow windows.

"What is it, Rosie? Would you like to meet Katie Kym and her dog Dudley? She has not come home yet."

Rosie Hip pondered for a while, then with shaky hands she pulled the golden nut out from her delightful woven basket. Faro took just one look at it, and his rubbery facial expression quickly changed, the smile disappearing. Hurriedly he cajoled her into the enchanting house.

"You must be very quiet about this, Rosie." He said. "The golden nuts are extraordinary."

Looking intensely at the golden nut he asked Rosie if the Hedgemen of Herefordshire had anything to do with this find.

"Yes." she replied.

He escorted Rosie into the ornate sitting room, there inside the wooden wonky house where not a single room was straight, where even the walls were curvaceously disorientating, he sat her down on an oversized chair and explained to her the importance of finding the golden nut. Then he noticed that the shell had been cracked on the nut - the secret was no longer inside!

"It is now very important that Katie Kym returns home quickly," he said. "She must be told at once. I will go and fetch her immediately. She has been placed in grave danger. The spores from opening the nut are highly toxic, highly poisonous; in the wrong hands they could be fatal."

Rosie Hip said that she had wanted to tell Katie Kym about the nut, but had promised not to tell a soul.

"Captain Privet and Commander Blackthorn will be angry." She said, "if they find out that I have now lost the secret of the golden nut."

Faro told Rosie not to worry too much because Katie Kym was not a stranger, unknown to them. Her family's ancestors for hundreds of years, had lived here in this place; this was Katie Kym's original home, here were her roots, the secret would be safe, if only it could now be found.

"Tomorrow, Rosie, I will call an urgent meeting in the folly - the one on the south side of the garden. Katie Kym will be able to provide us with the key, so we may all get in and discuss the future of the nut. In the meantime Rosie, you must contact all the Hedgemen of Herefordshire, by whatever means it takes."

Katie Kym had just finished crunching some of the autumn fruit, some of the bloated apples, pears and plums which she had unwittingly discovered in the garden that morning, while on her way to school. The new garden was full of surprises. Now she plucked a few more pieces of the delectable fruit, for Katie Kym could not get enough of the aromatic and addictive flavours of real, fresh fruit, dripping and oozing with the sweetest juices.

She continued to make her way back home. She noticed that the storm had cleared and she was spellbound by the beautiful rainbow which seemed to follow her all the way home. Yes, the rainbow had been following Katie Kym on her walk home! She had tremendous fun with the many-coloured shadows: one minute she was pink, then green, purple, yellow, orange, blue, unlike Rosie Hip, Katie Kym found this amusing, even fascinating. She was not in the slightest bit concerned about the tricks of nature. Sea School had been a good foundation, a good grounding for the unexpected. Yes, it was fun to be purple walking home!

She did not anticipate this funny-looking, multi-coloured talking man appearing from nowhere, as he walked side by side with her.

"What do you want?" Katie Kym inquired in a cool, casual, but stern and collected manner.

Faro had always admired earth's younger inhabitants. They were unspoilt innocents who got straight to the point, and Katie Kym was no exception. She had attitude and didn't care who knew it, she didn't care whatsoever about dishing out her dramatic indifferences from time to time, especially when the family debates got underway.

"Your name is Katie Kym, I believe? You are the Katie Kym who has just moved into the 15th century, wonky black and white house, are you not?"

"Yes, that is I," she replied. "And who are you, may I ask?"

"I am Faro. Now Miss Katie Kym, you must come with me. I have something important to explain to you."

Katie Kym turned around abruptly.

"I am most sorry, I do not mix with strangers, especially funny-looking, coloured ones like you, so buzz off and annoy somebody else, will you. I repeat buzz, with another buzz. Buzz off! I want to go home, so go away. Disappear, go back to rainbow land, or just buzz off and bother somebody else, you multi-coloured freak!"

But Faro had blocked the way, and Katie Kym could go no further. Faro had put a wall of colour in her path, so she could not move backwards or forwards.

"What have you done to me, you freak? Let me go home, or I will call the police on my mobile and tell them all about you, you idiot!" She shouted.

Now firmly trapped in Faro's multi-coloured, caged prism, and blinded by the beaming light, she was getting angry, extremely angry.

"Unless you listen to me, young lady, I will not let you go, do you hear? And for your information, my coloured capsule is soundproof. I cannot let you go because you have seen me now, and I an not going away, or as you say, Buzzing off. Only the bumble bee buzzes off, do you hear and understand Miss Kym?"

All this was getting a little heavy and intimidating for Katie Kym, though she did not show it. What did he really want she wondered? In the past, the sea creatures had been very dominating in their watery domain, but Katie Kym realised this funny-looking man was serious, so serious that he would not let her go out of the coloured bars. No alternative but to listen, she reasoned, listen to what he had to say, or else she would be stuck here forever, and she wanted to go home.

So Katie Kym listened carefully. She had been locked unwillingly inside Faro's beaming prism of powerful, coloured lights, but she fully understood now what he had to say, and she full understood why he had followed her home, and why he was staying at her new house.

She rushed home with the utmost urgency as soon as Faro released her, and was instantly shocked when she arrived and saw her new house.

What had that rainbow man done to the wonky house? Dad will have a fit when he sees this, she thought: The Rainbow Man has painted it all different colours. And she wondered what on earth her mother had been doing while all this painting had been going on. Why had she not stopped him? Yes, Dad was definitely going to have a fit.

Entering the house, Katie Kym saw that he had even painted all the rooms in different colours. She went straight to her mother's room, her mother's head was weaving away through some unpacked boxes. Katie Kym demanded to know if she had any idea what The Rainbow Man had done to their new house.

"Yes Katie, I am awfully aware, and he's done a lovely job. I could not have done it better myself."

Katie Kym was taken aback by her mother's laidback attitude. She just did not have a care in the world. She was right, this was a madhouse, a spooky, wonky, madhouse, where sanity did not prevail and rainbow men were allowed to paint the entire house in different colours.

In the sitting room she found Rosie Hip perched on the old wooden chair, a golden nut still in her basket, where she had been sitting and waiting for what seemed like hours, for Katie Kym .

Faro was standing in the bay window, he had promised to introduce Katie Kym to Rosie Hip in this cheerful room which now had bright yellow walls and a sky blue ceiling.

Katie Kym appeared overwhelmed by little Rosie Hip. Everything about her was so endearing. Katie Kym just loved her; she was so small, so pretty, so cute, so cute this talking little doll was fantastic, just what she had always wanted.

Rosie Hip was so tiny, Katie Kym picked her up very gently and placed her in the palm of her hand. Katie Kym could not believe her luck; seeing and meeting Rosie Hip gave her a wonderful surprise. She felt so special, so privileged, she would not let her new friend down, or out of her sight for a that matter.

Being absolutely thrilled, absolutely thrilled, Katie Kym was quick to show Rosie Hip her new bedroom. Rosie was aghast at all the strange looking implements, CD player, television, stuffed toys which looked almost real, she wondered why this clutter of the new, modern world was so important to Katie Kym. Rosie Hip, after all, managed to live outdoors without it.

Katie Kym then decided that it was time to escort Rosie Hip safely home, telling her that she had really enjoyed the evening they had spent together. Katie Kym now wanted to spend the night in Rosie Hip's house, but this was impossible, Rosie said, as her house was far to small for Katie Kym. They kissed each other and said goodnight, not wishing to be parted one from the other.

Chapter Four

~

Seven Blue Purses

Ding-a-ling, ding-a-ling! Ring-a-ding, ring-a-ding! Ding-a-ling, ding-a-ling! Mr Pole's bush telegraph services were in full demand this morning. The ding-a-ling, ring-a-ding bells, were used by him to contact the Hedgemen of Herefordshire.

Sipping homemade wild cherry mazzard juice, Rosie Hip could hear Captain Privet and Major Conker racing around, bellowing orders to the rest of the disorderly Hedgemen.

"Chivvy it, chivvy it, come along now, come along, Miss Hip! Are you ready, Miss Hip? Are you ready? Do you want me to come inside and get you?"

Rosie had no desire to attend Faro's forthcoming meeting with Commander Blackthorn. Most likely he would have immense pleasure marking her red coat with one of those anti-social thorns of his. The very idea put Rosie Hip into a real flapperty-flap. For the sake of her red coat, however, she decided not to have an argy-bargy with the prickly Commander. .

"No, no, no, Commander!" Rosie replied. "You carry on, I will see you later."

Rosie really did not like or trust him. She made a point of waiting for Mr Pole, as they had already planned to attend the meeting together, along with her new friend, Miss Katie Kym.

The golden nut had got everybody far too excited, too excited for their own good. They all needed to calm down and take stock of what was really happening, as they were being invaded from all directions.

Ding-a-ling-a-dong! Ding-a-ling-a-ding! Ding-a-ling-a-dong!

Mr Pole spent the entire morning rebuffing claims that a golden nut had been found. Mr Pole was always most discreet, you see. It would not do to inform the other villagers about the Hedgemen, about the golden nut. Rosie shuffled up to Mr Pole. She could hear that he had been engaged in a most troublesome and awkward conversation. Not a pleasant one, not a pleasant one at all. There were raised voices, raised voices on both sides.

"Madame, for the tenth time, the rumours circulating about a golden nut tree being found here are not only preposterous, not only stupid, not only ridiculous, but absolutely absurd! There is no such thing as a golden nut tree, or a golden nut!"

And he blasted down the almost worn-out wires: "Finally, Madame, may I bid you good day!"

Finally, Rosie Hip and Mr Pole were now able to take matters in hand. They were fully aware of the awkward squad, led by Prudence Potter and Betty Blackcurrant, who would not spare any one of them any mercy. They could all do without the local village jam-makers, as they made things even more complicated, even stickier than they needed to be.

Prudence Potter and Betty Blackcurrant were awful jam-makers. They would cheat with their fruit, which was never organic. The fruit grown on their farm was just pumped up with poisonous pesticides, which had eradicated a lot of other natural inhabitants who used to live in the countryside, eradicated by their chemical blitz. The Hedgemen had wanted to eradicate Potter and Blackcurrant. They had called them Nitro Betty and Phosphorus Pru, they were both as deadly as the chemicals they were using.

Rosie Hip had told Katie Kym all about her new neighbours. Rosie had warned Katie not to be tempted to eat the over-swelled strawberries or blackcurrants from that farm because of the fertilizers, pesticides and growth hormones, which they used to urge the quick growth of their fruit, Rosie Hip also warned her about the neighbouring stream and river. These had become a dumping ground for the chemical residues; even the water was not safe to drink. The other local farmers were sick and tired of the jam-makers. They all wanted them out, because they were affecting their animals and their small organic businesses, which had suffered losses as a result of the contamination.

Katie Kym, Rosie Hip and Mr Pole had now made their way to the very bottom of the long and winding garden. They entered the lovely folly, overgrown with ivy, ramshackled, and surrounded by late-budding wild flowers: bluebells, sunflowers and poppies.

Faro was already sitting at his desk, amidst the endless vines of ivy which shaded the room, looking seriously at the large wooden box in Katie's hands, looking seriously at them all. He asked Katie Kym to sit next to him and pass him the wooden box, which she had brought up from the house.

The carved satin-like wooden box had an unusual appearance. It had a rather large brass padlock, which hung from a shiny brass plate. Inside the padlock there was an enormous brass key. The brass key had a bright blue tassel, which had been tied to the round opener. This had been done so that the key could not be easily lost. It certainly looked most interesting, with the swaggering bright blue tassel.

Faro chaired the meeting, along with Katie Kym, who made notes. It had become obvious to everybody seated within the ramshackled folly that today was going to change their lives forever. So, they were all very apprehensive but also excited as Faro made his opening address.

"This must be the first time in a hundred years that a beautiful golden nut has been found in this part of Herefordshire," he said.

He explained to his audience, which included Rosie Hip, Mr Pole, Captain Privet, Major Conker, Commander Blackthorn and the Head Stickler, that finding the golden nut had created tremendous problems. Not only was it the first to be found in the area for such a long time, but it also meant that there must be others. It would no longer be safe to place the nut in the care of one pair of hands, especially those of Katie Kym or Rosie Hip, or indeed of any of them. Faro went on to explain that the whole village community would now be in danger because of outsiders entering the village. The chattering classes had become relentless in their endeavours to spread the rumours. There would be an immense amount of interest on the part of strangers arriving from far away places, seeking to find and steal, if they must, just to possess a golden nut.

"And this particular type of nut tree would have produced others," he said.

Faro had seen the very tree: the tree that had produced the golden nut. He had returned to it the previous evening, and collected the remaining golden nuts.

"On all nut-bearing trees, nuts normally grow in clusters," he explained.

But this one was very unusual. There were no clusters, and its twisted and curvaceous slender branches had glowed, as gold as the nuts. Then, once the nuts had been picked, the branches had reverted to a normal tree colour, which had been a relief to Faro. He had carefully collected the six other nuts, and placed each one separately into a blue velvet purse, which he had taken out of the wooden box. Then he had returned to the house, and the purses containing the golden nuts were put back into the box. To conclude the meeting, Faro opened the wonderfully imposing satin-like wooden box. The brass key clicked on all cylinders, and the box sprang open, the blue purses almost bursting out. They were all given one each.

Commander Blackthorn could not believe his luck. Once he had got hold of his blue purse, he started making plans of his own. Major Conker looked on, slightly disappointed not to be the first to receive a purse. Like Rosie Hip, he did not like or trust the Commander, and the Commander's face said it all.

Captain Privet of course was extremely delighted. Once a

captain always a captain, and he had no other desire but to remain a captain. A proud Captain, he had not expected it. Captains did not normally receive interesting gifts, especially nothing as thrilling as a blue purse containing a secret golden nut.

Mr Pole and Rosie Hip just stared in utter disbelief at each other, having been totally shocked that Faro had found the other nuts. Mr Pole intended to have a further discussion with Rosie Hip about this later.

The Head Stickler was most concerned about receiving a purse. He felt sure he would not be able to look after it properly, given that most of his family had now gone missing in the stream.

After giving all of them a purse each, Faro kept reminding them of the importance of not losing the nuts, including Katie Kym. Faro had felt quite safe about giving one to Katie Kym, as the one he gave her had not been opened and she would not be affected by the contents.

He concluded the meeting by telling each of them to be extremely careful; once again not to lose the purses, and to guard them safely until springtime. He made it quite clear that he would meet them all again in the springtime, all being well. And as it was now coming up to Christmas time, he suggested they should all have a party. Katie Kym's moving in was a great excuse for a party, and they would all be able to celebrate finding the golden nuts. After the party he would have to leave the house once again, and return home.

They all left the folly to return to their homes. And on the very next day, Katie Kym and Rosie Hip started the preparations for the Christmas Party. Katie made the most wonderful invitations, with Rosie Hip's guidance, but they were very selective as to whom they were sent. They called it the Christmas Nut Party.

Organising a party can be tremendous fun. Rosie Hip took Katie Kym on a garden outing, to collect the remaining winter goodies while they were still fresh. These included potatoes which, as Rosie Hip explained to Katie Kym, had grown underground. Of course, they can be pulled up any time, if you remember where they have been planted. They also picked the last of the winter fruits: apples, pears, late autumn raspberries, which were superb and a real treat for the time of year.

Rosie Hip promised Katie Kym that next year, when Faro had returned in the springtime, they would plant and grow lots more fruit and vegetables together. Katie was amazed. She found it a little hard to believe that the little seeds which Rosie Hip collected on their garden outing would by magic turn into lovely food. Rosie Hip's little basket was full to the brim with all sorts of different seeds. Katie Kym promised to put a few into flower pots, and to keep them indoors during the cold winter.

The seeds would provide them all with a bumper harvest next year, Rosie said.

Getting ready for the party, getting ready for Christmas: kept them busy for several days. Sampling the culinary delights was also very satisfying. Rosie's mazzard syrup and Katie Kym's wibbly-wobbly lovely-jubbly cranberry orange port jelly: both tasted as if they had been made in paradise! The chanterelle mushroom soup was the best ever, and the mazzard syrup made them all feel warm and sleepy.

Yes, the party was an outstanding success! The magic house looked even more enchanting, as winter snow had engulfed the entire village, covering every garden, including Rosie Hip. Rosie wished Katie Kym a very happy Christmas. Rosie explained to Katie that she would have to go to sleep for the remainder of the winter, in her own bed. Katie Kym was a little upset, because she would miss her dreadfully. Rosie said that winter is not as long as you think: she would be awake and fully refreshed eight weeks from Christmas day.

So they parted for a while. Rosie Hip was now safely tucked up in her winter house. The snow had not gone, but Christmas had. Katie Kym was counting the weeks: six more until Rosie Hip would wake up again!

One more week to go before the winter was finished! One more week before Katie Kym could meet up again with Rosie Hip! Katie had stayed awake for all of the winter, but today she felt tired. She went back to bed, and stayed there for the rest of the week.

Chapter Five

~

Blooming Springtime

Katie Kym had spent the last week in bed as she had been unwell. She had chicken pox, and was covered from head to toe with itchy red spots.

Rosie Hip had been seriously worried for her friend as the local doctor made frequent visits, which had alarm bells ringing everywhere. Gathering all the ingredients with her little basket, Rosie Hip spent an entire day preparing the cocktail that hopefully make Katie feel better, she proceeded to take it to Katie Kym's bedroom via the window route.

Splatter, splatter, clatter, clatter, splosh, wash, splosh, splatter, splosh, wash! Cotch ya! Cotch ya! Clatter bang wallop and splatter!

Rosie Hip needed to go out now despite the heavy rain, she too stayed indoors all through the winter and now it was time to go out to visit poorly Katie Kym. On the way there she noticed how quiet the garden was. There did not seem to be anybody about. She started to think that all her friends had moved away due to the hard winter. Or maybe, just maybe, it had been a little too early to wake up. Maybe, just maybe, it was a little too early to be reunited with her friends, for they could still be enjoying their long winter sleep.

Rosie Hip started to tissue, tissue, tissue! Clearly she was also becoming unwell. Slightly doubtful about going any further now, Rosie Hip took the opportunity to contact Mr Pole's bush telegraph service while she was outside his very tall house. It certainly had been a long time since they had had one of their discreet little tête-à-têtes. Yes, a little chatter would do no harm today, as he may be able to help her deliver Katie Kym's medicine. Ding dong, ding dong! Ding dong! Ding-a-long-a-dong!

"Mr Pole, Mr Pole, is that you?" Rosie inquired most politely.

"ROSIE! Rosie Hip! It's marvellous to hear from you! Come in if you want to."

"Mr Pole, I cannot stop for long. I have a herbal medicine for Katie Kym who unfortunately has been most unwell, and I have noticed how quiet the garden is. There is something I am a little unsure of, Mr Pole. May I inquire if I have woken up from the winter too early, as it seems to have gone by so quickly, and it still seems awfully mucky, yucky, wet and cold."

Mr Pole quickly assured Rosie Hip that she had not woken up too early, and that Katie Kym was on the mend as he had first-hand knowledge, because the doctor had also used his bush telegraph service.

Rosie Hip really did like Mr Pole. He always had so much to say that interested her. He was so clever to be able to store all this information, she thought, and she was so lucky to have him as a friend.

"In four days time, Rosie, Faro will return, in time for the final meeting concerning the golden nuts."

Mr Pole could see that Rosie had almost forgotten about their next meeting.

"Talking about the golden nuts, Rosie Hip, have you kept your blue purse safe?" he inquired. "Have you still got your golden nut? They've taken mine, you know."

Rosie Hip blinked. Blink, blink!

"Oh, the nut! Oh, the blue purse! Where have I put it? Where have I put it?"

Mr Pole had been right. She had completely forgotten about the blue purse; she had completely forgotten about the blue purse and the golden nut. Maybe, just maybe, she had woken too early, for she could not remember a thing.

Tissue, tissue, tissue!

Rosie Hip could not stop sneezing and tissuing. Mr Pole was very unclear as to who had stolen his purse and his prized golden nut. Every day for the last couple of months he had monitored all bush calls, just in case the thieves revealed themselves. Up to now this method of detection had been to no avail.

Rosie could not take any more of this. Her head was fuzzy muzzy, fuzzy muzzy, fuzzy muzzy. She felt awfully cold, then she was hot. Something had changed. What was wrong with Rosie Hip? Something was amiss, apart from her having a cold. She had not realised, you see, that now springtime had arrived, she had not only grown but had changed completely.

Rosie Hip outgrew her thick winter crimson red coat. She didn't have the slightest idea that now she had the most beautiful shimmering pure silk petal dress. The silky petal dress made of crimson pink, layer after layer, of silky crimson pink petals. Rosie Hip looked like a princess who was just about to go to a spring ball. As she walked the layered petals floated on the air around her. It had taken hundreds of petals to make such a beautiful dress.

Mr Pole was left speechless by Rosie Hip's sheer elegance, speechless as it was such a glamorous outfit to wear in the countryside, on a day like today. And speechless as to what Captain Privet might say. The Captain worried enough about her red coat, but this designer creation would certainly put him in a real tizzy dilemma. It was no wonder she caught a slight chill: the crimson silky pink petal dress was very delicate. Rosie went back home feeling dreadful. She lay on her bed, thinking about what Mr Pole had said. Slowly it all started to come back to her. She remembered the last time she had the blue purse. She definitely had no doubt about what she had done with her blue purse and the golden nut.

The Christmas Party, the Christmas Nut Party, the yellow mushroom chanterelle soup, the warm autumn aromatic mazzard syrup juice! They all got a little carried away; they all drunk and ate too much of everything.

Rosie Hip remembered being escorted home by Katie Kym, along with Mr Pole and Captain Privet. This being after Major Conker and Commander Blackthorn started airing their differences, in public of all places. Rosie Hip was disgusted with them. Their rural manners disappeared altogether, showing her up in Katie Kym's house.

Katie Kym firmly put her foot down. After all, the party was held in her home she would not tolerate any bad behaviour as this would spoil it for the next one. The differences were not settled at the party; they rumbled, and rumbled on, all the way to Rosie's house.

The constant squabbling happened because there was no way the sticklers could look after their blue purse; they were very worried about losing it.

Commander Blackthorn had complained bitterly that his troupe of thorny Hedgemen would do a better job of looking after the sticklers' blue purse. But Katie Kym did not forgive the

Commander for stabbing her with one of his black thorns. She had certainly given him his marching orders, to the point of asking him to leave the party early, and to vacate the wonky house.

Major Conker perfidiously defended his own squad; he argued that the Commander was the only thorny Hedgemen to protect the purse and the secret golden nut. Thorns the Commander may have, but the Major's squad, he insisted, had all the muscle, big muscles at that, needed to protect the blue purse and the golden nut from prying outsiders. Major Conker had a hard muscular shell, he would not back down on this issue whatsoever.

Rosie Hip intervened. She told Katie the Major could be trusted far more than the Commander. The Commander backed off, but his scorning, scratchy remarks soured the mazzard juice and soured the party, so they all left a little earlier than expected, to the relief of Mr Pole.

Mr Pole also warned Katie Kym and Rosie Hip about mixing the cocktails too much, but the pair had insisted it was a Christmas party. They were both in stitches as the cocktails started to take effect.

Rosie Hip and Mr Pole witnessed Betty Blackcurrant and Prudence Potter spying through the windows of the wonky house when the party started. Neither were invited, so they waited outside until the party had finished. Then they followed them home. The pair also witnessed the squabbling, enjoying every minute of it. Both of the jam-makers intervened, offering to help with this awful dilemma, almost to the point of threatening to tell the whole village about it, tell the whole village as to what had really been found.

Katie Kym, Rosie Hip and Mr Pole could not risk this, so they had deliberated, and after a lengthy meeting, they decided it would be best for all if the jam-makers did look after the sticklers' blue purse, just to keep them quiet, and shut them up for good.

Prudence Potter and Betty Blackcurrant did not wait too long before having a little nose into the contents of the purse.

"Oh, what have we here? A secret golden nut! Oh, just as we expected! Just as we heard!"

Yes, the rumours were true! The jam-making business, led by Potter and Blackcurrant, had been under-performing.

Potter and Blackcurrant realised that the golden nut had all the ingenious ingredients, natural and magical, that would produce the best organic mouth-watering, yummy, yummy food products. And the news about this yummy food spread like wildfire. Mothers went out shopping and queued if necessary to buy the latest products, the favourites being golden-coated chocolate nut biscuits, gold nut jam and gold nut bread.

All the previous claims of chemical intervention were truly disposed of, the golden nut had worked, they could do no wrong.

It did not take too long for Mr Pole's bush telegraph service to get a line and find out what had been going on. Mr Pole had been horrified: the ever-expanding business methods of Potter and Blackcurrant had confirmed his suspicions about them. They had tricked Captain Privet, they had tricked Commander Blackthorn, they had tricked the Major, tricked all the

Hedgemen into parting with their blue purses and golden nuts.

The result was that the production of new food products could be maintained at this mega-production level. Potter and Blackcurrant did not leave a nut tree standing. There was no longer a nut or a nut tree left in the village. Potter and Blackcurrant had blatantly stolen and used the lot. This meant that the wildlife including the birds had no food for the winter months. This was a disaster: no more nuts would ever grow again, and the red squirrel would be extinguished for ever, through lack of a natural nut diet.

Katie Kym and Rosie Hip had not been so foolish as to get involved with Potter and Blackcurrant. Like Mr Pole, they were frightened and horrified at what had been to done to their village, horrified with the sheer scale of destruction that had taken place all around them.

Once Mr Pole had got a line on the unscrupulous business dealings, he had contacted Rosie Hip at once. They both went to the edge of the village, and buried their two blue purses for safe keeping, not even realising that they had been followed.

Rosie Hip had no desire to exploit the secrets of the golden nuts. It was fairly evident by now that they could cause lots of problems if they were not used correctly. The nuts were supposed to make everyone happy, but clearly everything had turned into a nightmare.

Captain Privet, Commander Blackthorn, Major Conker and the sticklers, had all moped about through the winter months. At the time they felt that parting with their blue purses, parting with the golden nuts, was a good idea. The Hedgemen were now homeless after the destruction of their natural homes.

Clatter, clatter! Clatter bang, clatter bang! That swirling eye in the sky, the black cloud of a clatter banger, had once again darkened the whole village. Red, yellow, orange, blue, purple and green: whoosh, whoooosh!

Faro had returned. He made his way straight to the folly. They were all waiting for him with long sombre faces. Katie Kym did not attend as she had not yet made a full recovery; she had asked Mr Pole to pass a message to Faro, explaining her circumstances.

"Cheer up, cheer up, this is not the end of world!" said Faro.

They all looked up in disbelief.

"It is!" said Rosie Hip. "All the blue purses, all the golden nuts; they have gone, gone forever!"

Faro started tutting, tutting and tutting.

"I did warn you all before I left, that finding the golden nuts would cause immense problems, and that you would all have to be very careful.

Meanwhile, Faro had opened the satin-like wooden box. The blue purse had been taken from there too! He was very annoyed by what had happened, but he could do nothing now they had all gone. He had known that something like this would happen. Never mind, he thought, that's life.

He beamed his way into Katie Kym's bedroom, wondering where she had been all this time while the thieving had been going on. Chicken pox had left Katie Kym totally deflated, totally depressed. Faro could see that she had been very poorly; he had no idea how long she had felt this way. Sitting on the edge of the bed, making funny shapes with his coloured shadows, he tried to cheer her up.

Katie Kym looked very dazed, confused with the funny shapes, she sat up and welcomed him home with open arms. Bursting into floods of tears, she asked Faro to work his magic and get rid of all her spots; all she could think about was her ridiculous spots.

"What you need, young lady, is sunshine and fresh air. This room is dull and stale. The curtains are closed, the room needs to be aired and repainted."

Katie Kym started to smile; already he had cheered her up. She asked if Rosie Hip could help decorate her bedroom. Faro agreed. Then, in what seemed to be a flash, Rosie Hip and the Hedgemen were now in her bedroom. They were all very fed up about losing the golden nuts. Truly, Faro had returned home to the glums. Yes, he had renamed them the glums!

One by one, Faro insisted they put their hands in his pocket if they were to help decorate. Rosie did so, and laughed when her hand came out pink. The Captain's came out green, the Major's purple, Mr Pole's orange, the Commander's blue, and Katie Kym's red.

"Here we go! Let's do the rainbow shuffle", said Faro, fingers dripping with luscious bright colours. "This is how it's done: stand on a chair, put your hands and fingers on the wall, starting at the top, and with a wriggle slowly slide them down to the bottom."

They all took turns to do this. The results were colour strophic. Katie Kym's bedroom was now decorated in rainbow stripes. It looked very good, and quite easy to do really; easy when you can do the rainbow shuffle. Rainbow decorating is a must when you have a dull bedroom.

Katie Kym loved her new bedroom. Instantly she started to feel much better; much, much better. She went to her jewellery case and took out three blue purses. They were all amazed.

Faro was over the moon.

"Good girl!" he said. "Good girl! You really have looked after yours, Katie Kym."

Katie explained that the other two belonged to Mr Pole and Rosie Hip. They were a little perplexed as to how Katie had managed to get hold of them.

"It was quite easy really, Rosie. You have been asleep all winter, and I was unable to talk to you. Mr Pole kindly came to see me just before you were going to bury the nuts, and explained everything that had happened. After he left, I told my Dad what had been going on. Dad followed the pair of you, and once you had gone he recovered the hidden two blue purses. And of course I still had mine here; hence three blue purses."

Carefully Faro opened each blue purse, carefully he opened the secret nuts.

"Katie Kym, do not come close now I have opened the nut. The spores you see can be poisonous if they have got a bit mouldy. Fortunately these are perfect, just perfect for what I now have in mind. Come on, all of you, we have work to do. Come on, Katie Kym! Wrap up warm and come outside to get some fresh air."

They all left the bedroom, walked down the garden, Katie

holding on tightly to Rosie's hand, and made their way once again to the folly. Rosie Hip stopped with a jolt.

"What is it, Rosie Hip?" asked Katie Kym.

"My basket, I need my basket!"

The Captain quickly returned to Rosie's house and fetched the basket, returning it to her just as swiftly. They all went to the bottom of the very large garden, and started to plant the seeds that Rosie had collected in the late autumn of last year; these she had carefully stored in her basket. They all spent a lot of time on this; the seeds were planted one by one, row after row.

Faro was very pleased that Rosie Hip bothered to save the seeds, and he was very pleased that Katie Kym had managed to keep hold of the three purses. It was now time for him to return home. They all looked sad. The glums had returned, as Faro was a true friend. He said he had no choice because he had a lot of other work to do. Katie Kym asked him what could be done about the missing hedges, the Hedgemen's lost houses. Faro said that the jam-makers would close down now they had used up all their supplies. They had taken far too much last year, which had left them without any seeds for this year.

Faro took one last look at them all, holding the nuts tightly. He said his goodbyes, then started to twist, faster and faster. The ground around him started to spin, and then glowed brightly with his rainbow colours, spinning, spinning, high into the sky. Then he disappeared.

They all started to cry. The nuts had gone; now Faro had gone, still leaving the Hedgemen homeless. There was one almighty bang, and at once the biggest rainbow you have ever seen appeared. Faro could be seen sprinkling the secrets of the golden nuts all over the little village. Within seconds, the ground around them started to crackle and shake, crackle, shake and shake. All the missing hedges, all the missing nut trees, had been miraculously replaced. Everything had returned back to normal. This was the secret of the golden nuts.